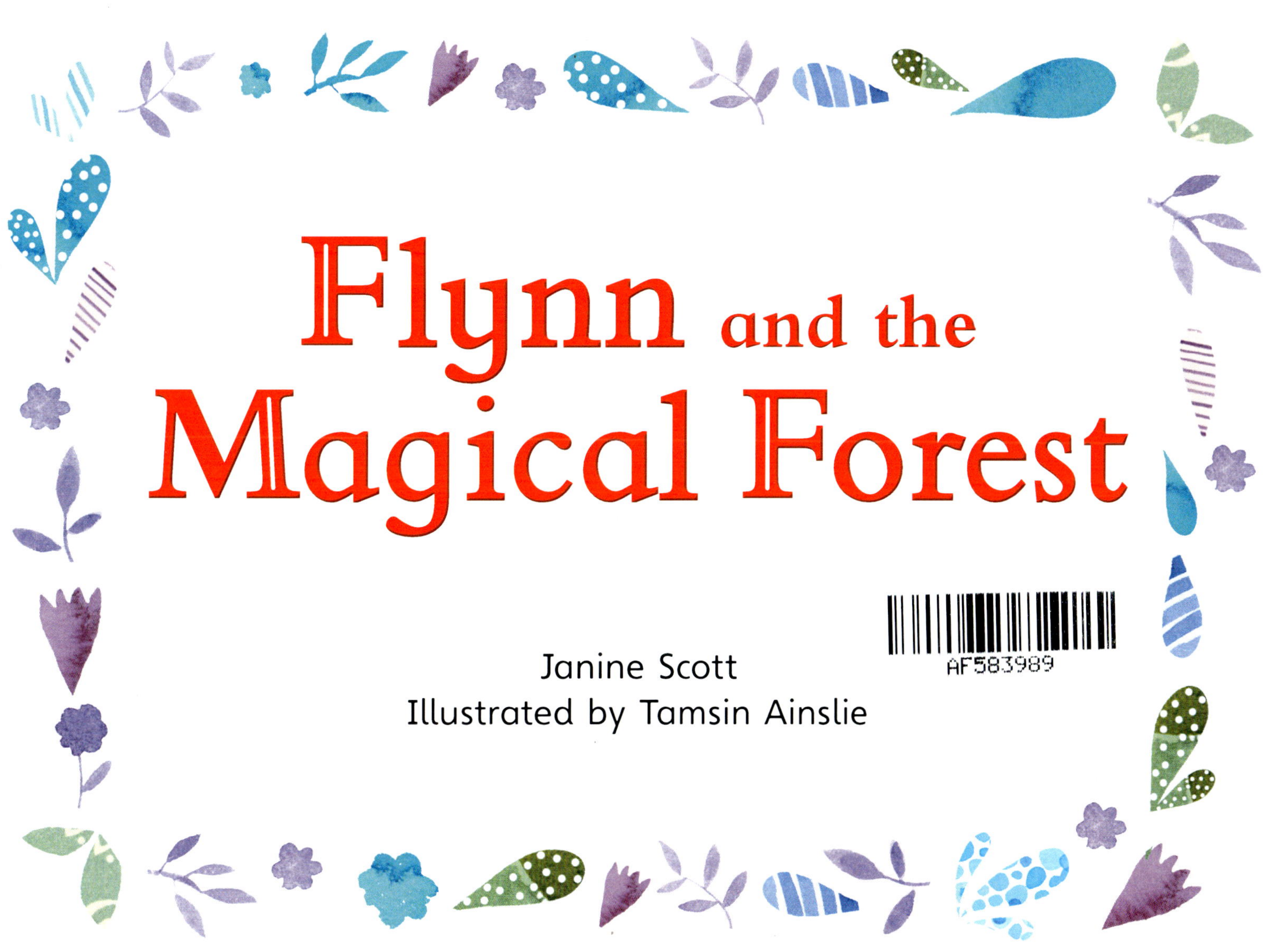

Flynn and the Magical Forest

Janine Scott
Illustrated by Tamsin Ainslie

Prince Flynn was walking home.
He was in a magical forest.

The forest was dark.
Flynn was lost.

Flynn saw a pink owl.
"Can you help me find
my way home?" said Flynn.

"No," said the owl.

Flynn saw a blue fox.
"Can you help me find
my way home?" said Flynn.

"No," said the fox.

Flynn saw a green rabbit.
"I am lost," said Flynn.
"Can you help me?"

"No," said the rabbit.
"I cannot help you."

Flynn saw a pink firefly.
“No one can help me!” he said.

“I can help you,”
said the firefly.

"I can light up the forest!"